New Canadian Kid

Invisible Kids

Also by Dennis Foon:

Plays

Chasing the Money
Kindness
Mirror Game
Rick: The Rick Hansen Story
Seesaw
Skin & Liars
War

Novels

Double or Nothing
Skud

The Longlight Legacy
The Dirt Eaters
Freewalker
The Keeper's Shadow

For more information visit www.dennisfoon.com

New Canadian Kid

Invisible Kids

2 Plays by

Dennis Foon

Playwrights Canada Press
Toronto

For professional or amateur production rights, please contact:
Michael Petrasek
Kensington Literary Representation
34 St. Andrew Street, Toronto ON M5T 1K6
416.848.9648, kensingtonlit@rogers.com

LIBRARY AND ARCHIVES CANADA CATALOGUING IN PUBLICATION
Foon, Dennis, 1951-
    New Canadian kid & invisible kids / Dennis Foon.
Plays.

New Canadian kid first published: Vancouver :Pulp Press, 1982
    Reissued with Invisible kids: Vancouver : Pulp Press, 1989.

ISBN 978-0-88754-830-7
    I. Title. II. Title: New Canadian kid and invisible kids. III. Title: Invisible kids.

PS8561.O62N483 2006   jC812'.54   C2006-904384-1

We acknowledge the financial support of the Canada Council for the Arts, the Ontario Arts Council (OAC), the Ontario Media Development Corporation, and the Government of Canada for our publishing activities.

Canada Council Conseil des arts
for the Arts   du Canada

ONTARIO ARTS COUNCIL
CONSEIL DES ARTS DE L'ONTARIO
an Ontario government agency
un organisme du gouvernement de l'Ontario

Canada

Ontario
Ontario Media Development
Corporation

New Canadian Kid

New Canadian Kid was first produced by Green Thumb Theatre for Young People in September, 1981 on tour in British Columbia, and at the Calgary International Festival for Young People, with the following company:

Mother	Kathryn Daniels
Nick	Robin Mossley
Mench	Wendy Noel
Mug	Colin Thomas

Directed by Jane Howard Baker
Set and Costumes by Sandy Cochrane

Staging Notes
Apart from the opening scene that takes place in Homeland, the entire action of the play occurs in Canada: a school classroom, playground, and the home and porch of Nick's family.

After much experimentation, I have come to the conclusion that with this play, simplest is best: the set should consist of a free-standing window that represents the home interior. Covered with a blackboard, it serves as a backdrop for the school scenes. Three stools may be used by the kids in the classroom scenes. Mother may use a chair that sits by the window. If you feel extravagant, treat yourself to a Canadian flag that may stand upstage.

The colour of Homeland is green. Nick and his mother should be dressed completely in shades of green, in contemporary store-bought clothing, there is a very important reason for this: the Homelanders should look alien to the Canadians—and to the audience, but their costumes should not be identifiable to any specific country.

The Canadian should be dressed in other primary colours: colours that Nick may later integrate into his costume as he becomes more comfortable in Canada, such as when he receives clothing. The audience should identify with them from their first entrance, so their costumes should be very similar to what the audience finds acceptable and appealing.

Players
MOTHER, a woman from Homeland
NICK, her son
MENCH, a Canadian girl
MUG, a Canadian boy

Setting
The Present.

The Jibberish
Because the play is attempting to show the audience what it is
like to be in a country without the same language or customs, the
Homelanders speak English and the Canadians speak jibberish, a
kind of language invented by the actors in each production based
on the dialogue I provide.

The original jibberish was created by Colin Thomas and Wendy
Noel, and since that first production it has been constantly
modified and updated by myself and other actors. So the jibberish
in this script has been evolving for twenty-five years, a necessary
process because the jibberish should include local and topical
references. Use the jibberish in this text as a launching off point,
inventing a completely new language if you want.

NICK addresses the audience.

NICK   My name is Nick. I come from a country called
                Homeland. But now I live in Canada.

MOTHER   *(off)* Nick!

NICK   Coming…. The day I left Homeland, I said goodbye
                to my friends. I told them I'd write, that I'd come
                back soon.

MOTHER   *(off)* Nick!

NICK   …They gave me this lunch bowl as a going away
                present. I like my friends a lot. It was hard to say
                goodbye.

MOTHER   *(entering)* Come on, Nick, you haven't finished
                packing.

NICK   I was saying goodbye to my friends. Look what they
                gave me.

MOTHER   That's beautiful, Nick. We'll have to pack it really
                carefully. Now come on, Dad's waiting for us.

NICK   Mom, do we have to go?

MOTHER   Nick, we've talked about this already.

NICK   I want to talk about it again.

MOTHER   It's going to be okay. Canada's going to be good for
                all of us.

NICK   I don't want to leave my friends.

MOTHER   You'll make new ones. Everything's going to be new.
                Even the language—English.

NICK   English? It'll be like learning to talk all over again.

MOTHER   No, it won't even take a week. You'll love Canada.
                Let's go.

NICK   Canada. So far away. I'd seen airplanes before
                but I'd never been in one. I was scared at first,

everything was shaking. But then we were up in the sky. I missed a half hour of it though—accidentally I locked myself in the washroom.

When we landed, we were in Canada. It was winter, really cold. My very first day in Canada, I licked some snow from a frozen fence post and my tongue got stuck. Later, after we found a place to live, I started to go to school.

> *MENCH, a Canadian girl, enters. She brings her stool downstage. She is listening to her iPhone, dancing to the beat, singing a current pop hit in jibberish. As her outrageous performance peaks, MUG, a Canadian boy, enters. He picks up his stool and places it next to hers. She is too involved in her show to notice him. MUG is amused and mimics her behind her back. Finally he lifts the headphone off one of her ears.*

MUG   Lo, Mencha. [Hi, Mench.]

MENCH   Lo, Mog. [Hi, Mug.]

> *MUG parodies MENCH's singing and dancing. She chases him. MUG suddenly stops at the blackboard. Written on it are some math problems titled: "Homvorko Matmatiko"*

MUG   Ah, poopit! Es sue kwit vos homvorko? [Oh crud! Did you finish your homework?]

MENCH   Yo. [Yes.]

MUG   Givva may. [Give it to me.]

MENCH   Nax. [No.]

MUG   Aw, moose. [Aw, come on.]

MENCH   Costa. [It'll cost you.]

MUG   Einst queenie coin. [A quarter.]

MENCH   Nax. [No.]

MUG   Doost queenie coin. [Two quarters.]

MENCH   Sue-she. [Okay.]

> She takes the money. MUG starts copying the work
> from her notebook into his. MENCH nervously
> watches for the teacher.

Zapit! [Hurry up!]

MUG   Ee bee! [I am!]

MENCH   Zap zapit! [Move it!]

MUG   Vor shure! [Alright!]

MENCH   (going to him) Givva may. [Give it to me.]

MUG   Nax. [No.]

MENCH   Kwit? [What?]

MUG   Doost queenie coin. [Two quarters.]

MENCH   Ee finko Mastah Tuto. [I'll tell the teacher.]

MUG   Einst queenie coin. [One quarter.]

MENCH   Sue-she. [Okay.]

MUG   (taking the money) Audio vos headshnet? [Can I listen
             to your iPhone?]

MENCH   Einst queenie coin. [One quarter.]

MUG   Sue-she. [Okay.]

MENCH   Vo nax cronkit, Goobo. [Don't break it, goof.]

MUG   Ee nax cronkit, Boofo. [I won't break it, bozo.]

> He listens, stops.

Nax da volumo, Mencha. Turnst da ono. [No
volume, Mench. Turn it on.]

> MENCH turns it up all the way. MUG yowls. She
> turns it down. He starts to get into the music.

Ohh yo... [Oh yeah...]

> MUG *now begins his own performance, in jibberish, to a different current hit rock song. As his gyrations peak, NICK enters, carrying his bowl. MUG doesn't see NICK and continues. MENCH does and starts to giggle. Then MUG notices NICK and stops, embarrassed. But then, recovering, he jokes with MENCH, pointing at NICK who is dressed in the green colours of Homeland.*

Gander chay: Kermit da Froglet! [Look at him: Kermit the Frog!]

MENCH   *(to NICK)* Sue vancha rumpabum? Stat. [You want a stool? There.]

> NICK *does not understand.*

(pointing to a stool) Rumpabum! [Stool!]

MUG & MENCH Rumpabum! [Stool!]

> NICK *starts to get the idea and goes to the stool.*

MENCH   *(indicating that it is supposed to be downstage like theirs)* Nax. Parkit! [No. Put it there!]

> NICK *does and sits.*

Lo. Ee noma Mencha. Kay vo? [Hi. My name is Mench. What's yours?]

> NICK *does not reply.*

MUG   Chay noma Mencha! Kay vo! [Her name is Mench! What's yours!]

NICK   I don't understand.

MUG   *(mimicking NICK)* Ah don unnerstan.

> MENCH *laughs.*

Sue es Homelander, nax? [You're a Homelander, aren't you?]

NICK	Excuse me?
MUG	*(slowly)* Homeland.
NICK	Oh, yes. I am from Homeland.
MUG	*(mimicking NICK)* Ooo yas, I am frum Homeland.

MUG laughs at his own joke. MENCH joins in. NICK smiles.

MENCH	Ee noma Mencha. Mencha. [My name is Mench. Mench.]
NICK	Oh. Your name is Munch. You're Munch.
MUG	*(correcting NICK)* Mencha.
NICK	Mencha.
MENCH	Chay Mog. [His name's Mug.]
NICK	Muck.
MUG	*(irritated)* Mog!
NICK	Mog!... My name is Nick.
MENCH	Snick.
NICK	No, just Nick.
MENCH	Just Nick.
NICK	Nick. Nick!
MENCH	Nicknick.

MUG & MENCH
Nicknicknicknicknick!

MUG and MENCH stand up and begin singing "O, Canada" in jibberish. NICK is bewildered.

Bo Nadacan
Vo has et terrid bland
Lo parrot bleak
Ein toto boyo sand

MENCH   *(seeing that NICK is still seated)* Shtanten! [Stand up!]

MUG   Shtanten!

NICK   I'm sorry, I don't speak English yet. Not for another week.

MUG & MENCH
              (singing) Mik sheeny pumps
              Nos gander zam
              Oh yoyo maypo tree

MUG   Shtanten, boof! Shtanten—como dis! [Stand up, you goof! Stand—like this!]

              MUG demonstrates.

MUG & MENCH
              (singing) Bo Nadacan
              Nos shtanten gro
              Por tee
              Bo Nadacan
              Nos shtanten gro
              Por tee

              At the end of the song, NICK stands. MUG and MENCH sit.

MUG   Perfecto! [Perfect!] Ee nama saluto de Maypoleepo. [Now we salute the flag.]

              MUG makes a ridiculous gesture. NICK is skeptical and looks to MENCH, who quickly copies MUG. NICK then decides to follow. MUG now does a strange march around his stool. MENCH copies him. NICK follows. MUG puts his face down on his stool. MENCH does too. NICK shrugs and goes along with it. As soon as NICK has his face down, MUG and MENCH break their pose and sit. They stifle their laughter for a moment, but then it is too much and they crack up. NICK looks, realizes what has happened, and sits down. MUG and MENCH now begin their homework. MUG takes out a calculator.

Ay, Mencha, chaka may lock-you-bent-or. [Hey, Mench, check out my calculator.]

MENCH   Kwan sue score it? [Where'd you get it?]

MUG   May moom-eye ee pop-eye. [My mom and dad.]

MENCH   Marzipan. [Excellent.]

MUG   Ver shure. [For sure.]

NICK   That's a nice calculator.

MUG   ...Homelanders nax hab lock-you-bent-ors. [Homelanders don't have calculators.]

MENCH   Sue jesto. [You're joking.]

MUG   Nax jesto. [For sure.] Gander dis, Homee! [Look at this, Homie!]

> *MUG and MENCH go to the blackboard. MENCH reads the math problem and MUG punches it into his calculator.*

MENCH   Saskatoon moosh rubiks da sublock dim sum: [Sixty divided by forty subtracted by twelve equals:]

MUG   Kalamazoo. [Eleven.]

> *MENCH checks her notebook against MUG's solution.*

MENCH   Nax correcto. Attempto encoro. [Wrong. Try again.] Saskatoon moos rubiks da sublock dim sum:

MUG   Kalamazoo.

MENCH   Nax correcto encoro. [Wrong again.]

NICK   You're pushing the wrong button.

MENCH   Nicknick, sue vancha trot da lock-you-bent-or? [Nick, you want to try the calculator?]

NICK   What?

MENCH   *(to MUG)* Al chay trotit. [Let him try it.]

MUG   Ein Homelander trotmay lock-you-bent-or. [Yes, let a Homelander try your calculator.]

Yo? [Yeah?]

MENCH   Yo. [Yeah.]

MUG   Yoyo. [Okay.]

> *MUG gives it to MENCH, MENCH hands it to NICK.*

NICK   I can try it?

MUG   Nax cronkit. [Don't break it.]

MENCH   *(to NICK)* Saskatoon moosh rubiks de sublok dim sum:

> *NICK finishes the problem quickly as she reads it. He shows her the answer on the calculator. She checks.*

...Correcto. [Right.]

MUG   Gibba may. [Give it to me.] Ee deeit, gibba may! [I said, give it to me!]

> *MUG grabs for the calculator, knocking it out of NICK's hand. It falls to the ground. MUG picks it up, checks it.*

Ee be crookee. Ee bee toot a crookee. [It's broken. It's totally broken.]

NICK   I didn't do it on purpose, I...

MUG   Chay cronko mein lock-you-bent-or. [He broke my calculator.]

NICK   I'm sorry, I didn't...

MUG   Mootard! [Idiot!]

MENCH   Et mo gander shtat. [Let me see that.]

> *She takes the calculator, bangs it on a stool.*

MUG   Oy! [Hey!]

MENCH   Bom. Ee bee sue-she nama. [Done. It's fixed now.]
         Gander. [Look.]

> *She hands it to MUG. He checks it, and sighs with
> relief. He then turns angrily to NICK:*

MUG   Sue nax toucha mein lock-you-bent-or encoro! [Don't
         you touch my calculator again!]

> *The bell rings. MENCH and MUG start to exit.*

MENCH   Nax Nicknick blan. [It wasn't Nick's fault.]

MUG   Homelander blan ver shur. [It was the Homelander's
         fault for sure.]

> *After MUG and MENCH exit, NICK addresses the
> audience.*

NICK   I didn't break it after all—it was okay. Mencha fixed
         it. And what a great calculator.

> *MENCH enters.*

MENCH   Munch mow-er. [Lunchtime.]

NICK   Munch mow-er?

> *She points to her mouth and exits.*

         Oh, lunchtime, great. *(to audience)* I keep my lunch
         in this bowl my friends gave me. In Homeland we
         say that the bowl keeps food and the food keeps life.
         I like to think of my friends. Hey, wait for me!

> *NICK runs off. MENCH and MUG enter with
> their lunches and sit.*

MUG   *(Pulling out a sandwich, he grimaces.)* Gahh. Sardeenos
         mik wheezechiz. [Sardines with cheezwhiz.]

MENCH   *(revealing a Big Mac)* Fridgo grosta mac. [Cold Big
         Mac.]

> *They put their sandwiches back into their lunchboxes in disgust. MUG finds something in his.*

MUG   Wo Yoyo! May Moom-eye pack ein grosta Hershee. Whacko! [Wicked! My mom packed me a giant Hershey. Excellent!]

> *He's in seventh heaven. He takes a bite of the chocolate and groans ecstatically. MENCH watches him hungrily. MUG notices.*

...Sue vanchen chunken, Mencha? [You want a piece, Mench?]

MENCH   Yoyo! [Yes!] *(She takes a bite.)* Taka. [Thank you.]

> *MUG opens the wrapper and sees a gigantic bite in his chocolate.*

MUG   Porko! [Pig!]

> *MENCH smiles at him sheepishly. NICK enters. They watch him. He sits.*

Sue tinker chay vanchen chunken? [Do you think he wants a piece?]

MENCH   Ver shure. Gibba Nicknick chunken da hershee. [For sure. Give Nick a piece of chocolate.]

MUG   Nicknick? Nax vay. [Nick? No way.]

MENCH   Oh, moose. [Oh, come on.] *(to NICK)* Nicknick, sue vantcha chunken da hershee. [Do you want a piece of chocolate?]

NICK   I don't understand.

MUG   Ee bay hershee. Sue nax condo kwit hershee set? [This is chocolate. Don't you know what chocolate is?]

MENCH   Gibba Nicknick bo chunken. [Give Nick a piece.]

MUG	Nax. [No.]
MENCH	Sue gibba mo encora chunken? [Will you give me another piece?]
MUG	Sue-she. [Okay.] Itsee bit. [Just a bit.]
MENCH	*(taking it)* Ver shure. [For sure.]

        MENCH runs over to NICK with the chocolate.

MUG	Oy! [Hey!]
MENCH	*(to NICK)* Tastay. [Taste it.]

        NICK takes it cautiously.

NICK	This looks like chocolate.
MENCH	Tastay. [Taste it.]

        NICK tentatively nibbles on it.

NICK	It is chocolate. I've never seen chocolate wrapped like this! Thanks a lot.
MENCH	Sue bettersket. [You're welcome.]
NICK	*(to MUG)* Thank you very much, Mug.

        *MUG smiles back at NICK, then taking the candy
        back from MENCH, wipes off the chocolate where
        NICK bit it. NICK does not see this because he has
        taken the lid off his bowl and begins eating from it.
        MUG puts his candy away, then sniffs the air.*

MUG	Kwesta fumo? [What stinks?]
MENCH	Kumquat fumo? [What stink?]
MUG	Sue nax sniffo da fumo? [You don't smell that stink?]

        MENCH sniffs, then grimaces.

MENCH	Yo yo. [Oh yeah.]
MUG	Ee bee huey. [I'm sick.]
MENCH	Ee bee spewy. [I'm really sick.]

MUG   Oy, Homelander—sue sniffo da fumo? [Hey, Homelander, you smell that stink?]

NICK   I don't understand.

MENCH   *(indicating that he should sniff)* Snaffa whifto—ee bee grosta kaka. [Take a whiff—it's really gross.]

NICK   You want me to smell something? *(sniffs)* I don't smell anything.

MUG   Lowd—ee bee grow dee. Ein fido musta poopit. [Lord—it's horrible. A dog must have pooped.]

> *MUG checks his shoes.*

Nax stompen may bootee. Chaw kay vos bootee, Mencha. [There's nothing stuck to my shoes. Check your shoes Mench.]

> *MENCH checks hers. They're clean and she sighs with relief.*

MENCH   *(to NICK)* Chaw kay vos bootee, Nicknick.

NICK   My shoes? *(He checks, they're clean. He shows them.)*

MENCH   Nax.

> *Meanwhile, MUG has been sniffing all around, attempting to trace the smell. Finally, he leans over NICK's bowl, sniffs, and jerks away.*

MUG   Oy, oy! Ee bee chay gorda! Ee bee munch da Nicknick. [Hey, hey! It's his bowl. It's Nick's lunch.]

MENCH   Sue jesto. [You're kidding.]

MUG   Yo, ver shure. Snifot. [Yes, for sure. Smell it.]

NICK   Hey, what's bugging you guys? I'm trying to eat my lunch.

> *MENCH sniffs NICK's bowl and gasps.*

MENCH   Kay bee shtat, Nicknick? [What is that, Nick?]

NICK   Does this smell bother you? It's just a seasoning, like
            salt. I don't know how you eat food without it.

MUG   Ee vanna corpso! [I want to die!]

NICK   You don't have to make those faces. If you tasted it,
            you'd probably like it.

MUG   Chay vanch may tastay? [Does he want me to taste
            it?]

MENCH   Goo fo shtat. [Go for it.]

MUG   Sue vanch may tastay? [You want me to try it?]

NICK   Yeah, here. Taste it.

MUG   Nax. [No.]

MENCH   Oo, chargit, nerd noggin. Tastay. [Oh, come on, big
            mouth. Taste it.]

MUG   (angrily) Nax, taka, Mencha!! [No thanks, Mench!!]

MENCH   Ooooo. Nicknick, Mog ein igg squirter. [Ooooo.
            Nick, Mug's a chicken.]

MUG   ...Sue she. [Alright then.] Skay may doma dis? [How
            do I do this?]

NICK   Just take a little bit like this.

            *NICK demonstrates, holding a little food with his
            thumb and index finger.*

            See? Just take a little bit in case you don't like it.

            *MUG takes a bit in his fingers with much disgust
            and trepidation. Suddenly he turns and shoves the
            food he's holding at MENCH, who jumps away.
            They laugh. Then MUG turns serious, saying to
            MENCH:*

MUG   See ee corpso, ditto mee moom-eye et pop-eye. [If I
            die, tell my mom and dad.]

MENCH   *(solemnly)* Bo bo. Tra la. Bee bee. [Goodbye. Good luck.]

> *MUG takes the tiny amount in his fingers and places it in his mouth. Slight pause. He seems to enjoy it. But then he starts to react: he goes into convulsions, he is gasping and screaming. He is hamming it up for MENCH and she loves it. Finally, after many death rattles, groans, and spasms, he is "dead." MENCH takes his pulse and pronounces him "dead."*

Chay corpso. [He's dead.]

> *Suddenly MUG is up again. The dead have risen; he is a horrible ghoul.*

MUG   Ee bee Zombo! [I'm a Zombie!]

> *He is a walking corpse, sniffing the air angrily.*

Ee vancha de gourda da Nicknick… Ee vancha da gourda da Nicknick. [I want the bowl of Nick… I want the bowl of Nick.]

> *Before NICK can react, MUG has grabbed the bowl and holds it over his head.*

Sisco la glowba. Corpsa la gourda da Nicknick! [Save the world. Kill the bowl of Nick!]

> *MUG bends the bowl on top of his head. It breaks in two. He is startled for an instant but quickly sees the humour in it, and gets MENCH laughing too.*

NICK   You broke it!

MUG   Gros bos. [Big deal.]

> *MUG tosses the pieces to NICK.*

MENCH   Ee bee joost ein gourda, Nicknick. [It's just a bowl, Nick.]

NICK   You broke my bowl.

MUG	Aw, post a itsi Nicknick. [Oh, poor little Nick.]
NICK	You don't know what that was, you idiot!
	NICK grabs MUG, MUG throws NICK on the floor.
MUG	Sue es logo. Toota des Homelander say logo. Sue Sgak. [You're crazy. All the Homelanders are crazy. You Sgak.*]
MENCH	*(shocked)* Mog!
MUG	Sgak!
	MUG exits.
NICK	...He broke my bowl.
MENCH	Donax regretto. Mog joost tantra. [Don't worry about it. Mug just got mad.]
NICK	Why did he do that?
MENCH	Or bay sue-she? [Are you okay?]
NICK	That was my good bowl.
MENCH	Ee besta zet nama. Tra la. [I'd better go now. Bye.]
	MENCH exits.
NICK	*(to the audience)* I just went home. I didn't wait for school to get out. I just left.
	NICK's mother enters and sits by the window. NICK looks in at her through the window, then decides to go in, hiding the broken bowl.
MOTHER	Oh, you're home, Nick. Hi.
NICK	Hi.
MOTHER	How was your first day of school?
NICK	Okay.
MOTHER	Meet any nice kids?

*Sgak represents a variety of cultural/racial slur words infamous in the English vocabulary.

NICK	Sure, lots.
MOTHER	You must be doing well in school, they let you out early.
NICK	Yeah, they let me out early.
MOTHER	What's that?
NICK	What?
MOTHER	That.
NICK	What?
MOTHER	That. In your hand.
NICK	Nothing
MOTHER	Nick.
NICK	A bowl.
MOTHER	That's the bowl your friends in Homeland gave you.
NICK	Yeah.
MOTHER	How did it get broken?
NICK	Dropped it.
MOTHER	You dropped it. How?
NICK	I dunno. Playing.
MOTHER	What happened?
NICK	I fell in the playground.
MOTHER	How did you fall?
NICK	I slipped.
MOTHER	Slipped. On what?
NICK	On a... a... banana peel.
MOTHER	Are you telling me the truth?
NICK	Yes.

MOTHER   Come over here, young man, and look me in the eye.

NICK   Mom.

> *NICK goes to her and she looks him in his eyes.*

MOTHER   Okay. Now say it.

NICK   I slipped on a banana peel.

MOTHER   Nick, why are you lying to me?

NICK   I'm not lying. You're the one who lied.

MOTHER   Nick, come one.

NICK   You told me I could learn to speak English in a week. It'll take forever! They talk so fast—blah, blah, blah—I don't even know what they're saying, I don't know what they want. Everything you said about this place was lies!

MOTHER   ...Nick, what's the matter?

NICK   Do you know what Sgak means?

MOTHER   Sgak. I don't know.

NICK   It's a bad word.

MOTHER   I don't know. Where did you hear it?

NICK   I was in a fight and this guy called me...

MOTHER   A fight? Did anyone get hurt?

NICK   No, this kid hates me. I hate him. I hate school. I hate Canada. I wanna go home.

MOTHER   I'm sure he doesn't hate you.

NICK   How do you know, were you there?

MOTHER   It's your first day at school. Remember, you're as strange to them as they are to you, right?

NICK   Yeah.

MOTHER	So if anyone bothers you, just ignore them. And Nick?
NICK	What?
MOTHER	I'll fix your bowl.
NICK	Okay.
MOTHER	Okay.

MOTHER exits.

NICK   *(to audience)* So the next day, I went back to school but I wasn't very happy about it. I just did what Mom said and tried to ignore them.

Enter MENCH with a bag of sports equipment. NICK turns away, ignoring her.

MENCH   Lo, Nicknick. Sue vancha planch? [Hi, Nick. Do you want to play?]

She notices that his back is turned from her and that he is looking up. She goes over to him and tries to see what he's looking at.

Kel gander shtat? Kel Matso? Nicknick? [What are you looking at? What's the matter? Nick?]

She goes back to her sports bag, going through some of the things inside.

Ee brognay gorbso sportso eekwippo. Gander. Ein, doos, tweet... [I brought gobs of sports equipment. Look. One, two, three...]

NICK continues to ignore her.

(in frustration) Sue nax vancha planch, sue nax vancha planch. [Well, if you don't want to play, you don't want to play.]

She gives up and sneaks behind NICK. NICK turns around and doesn't see her. Thinking MENCH has left, NICK goes to her sports bag. MENCH shadows him. He looks inside the bad, takes out a baseball. As he takes it out, he notices that MENCH is hiding behind him. He stands up and walks in intricate circles, making MENCH struggle not to be seen. He tosses the ball back and forth, making her run frantically as she tries to keep up with him and not be seen. Finally he throws the ball behind him and MENCH inadvertently catches it, revealing herself. NICK looks at her. They both laugh.

Lo, Nicknick. [Hi, Nick.]

NICK Lo, Menchamencha. [Hi, Menchmench.]

MENCH Nax. [No.] *(holding up one finger)* Mencha.

NICK Nax. [No.] *(holding up one finger)* Nick.

MENCH Nick?

NICK Nick.

MENCH *(hitting herself on the head)* Ohhh, yo.

NICK Yo.

MENCH *(handing NICK the glove)* Ee bee gerse glob glubber, Nick. [This is a baseball mitt, Nick.]

NICK Gerse glob glubber.

MENCH Bay perfecto! Nama... [That's perfect! Now...]

> *MENCH throws the ball. NICK catches it barehanded.*

Nax. Sue usta gerse glob glubber por kitz da gerseglob. [No. You use the baseball mitt to catch the baseball.]

NICK I understand...

> *MENCH notices that NICK hasn't even put the mitt on.*

MENCH   Nax, dos finger eight donk inksta gerse glob glubber.
           Cor cheesy. [No, your fingers go inside the glove.
           Like this.]

NICK   Cor cheesy? [Like this?]

MENCH   Yo. [Yes.]

> *MENCH throws the ball again. This time, NICK*
> *tries to use the mitt to hit the ball and sends it*
> *flying.*

           Nax, nax, sue usta gerse glob glubber por kitz da
           gerseglob. Nax shlam shtat. [No, no, you use the
           baseball mitt for catching the ball. Not hitting it.]

> *She demonstrates.*

NICK   I understand.

MENCH   Ay? [Eh?]

NICK   Oh. Yo, yo! [Yes, yes!]

MENCH   Sue-she. [Okay.]

> *MENCH throws NICK a pop-fly. NICK catches it.*

           Kwee-sin-art! [Excellent!]

NICK   Yo! [Yeah!]

MENCH   Kitz! [Catch!]

NICK   Bliss-tex! [Alright!] *(to audience)* So I started to make
           friends. I learned how to catch popshees...

> *He catches a fly ball.*

           ...and throw gutter globs...

> *He throws MENCH a ground ball.*

           ...and how to put someone out at first...

> *He catches the ball and tags out an imaginary*
> *runner.*

MENCH   Sewer rat! [You're out!]

NICK   And I learned how to play shlamshtick.

> MENCH hands NICK a hockey stick and they both pretend to skate, passing the invisible puck back and forth.

MENCH   Nama! [Now!] *(She passes to NICK.)*

NICK   Spinarama! [Turnaround!] *(NICK shoots.)* Chay chost! Chay shlamit! Chay scoro! [He shoots! He scores!] Yo! Ee bee Grain Wetsky! [Yeah! It's Wayne Gretzky!]

> They slap hands triumphantly, then hold hands in pain.

(to audience) And I learned to eat good Canadian foods, like—

> MENCH throws a basketball to NICK.

MENCH   Baykee Lassee!

NICK   *(catching the ball)* Hot dogs! *(He throws it back.)*

MENCH   Grosta Mack! *(throws it to NICK)*

NICK   Hamburgers! *(throws it back)*

MENCH   Greesee spudniks! *(throws to NICK)*

NICK   French fries! *(throws it back)*

MENCH   Chubbee blubber! *(throws to NICK)*

NICK   Double Bubble! *(throws it back)*

MENCH   Tweet shtay mik freezee moomoo mik cheetah chumps mik bakee sludge mik wing wong mik snikker giggle la tip top.

> She throws to NICK.

NICK   Three scoops of ice cream with bananas, hot fudge, peanuts, sprinkles…

> He throws the ball to MENCH.

...and a giant Snickers bar on top.

> *MENCH throws the ball back, it hits him in the stomach. NICK groans.*

And stomach aches... and I got a Nickee Jocko.

> *MENCH helps him put on a nylon jacket that has an adapted Nike logo.*

I was doing pretty good. And my English? I could speak...

MENCH   Sue-she. [So-so.]

> *MUG enters, carrying a baseball bat. He ignores NICK.*

MUG   Lo, Mencha. [Hi, Mench.]

MENCH   Lo, Mog. [Hi, Mug.]

> *MUG and MENCH play with the bat, gripping it hand over hand.*

NICK   Hi, Mug.

> *MUG ignores NICK.*

MUG   Checka may gerseglob gipper. Sue vancha pranta boont, Mencha? [Check out my bat. Want to practice bunting, Mench?]

MENCH   Sue-she, mo kitza. [Okay, I'll catch.]

NICK   Mo tossta! [I'll pitch!]

MUG   Nax. [No.]

MENCH   Ay? [What?]

MUG   Nax mit chay. [Not with him.]

MENCH   Kway nax? [Why not?]

MUG   May popeye dichay nax plancha mit chay. [My dad said not to play with him.]

MENCH	Sue popeye? [Your dad?]
NICK	Your dad won't let you play with me? Why not—kway nax?
MUG	Porska. [Because.]
MENCH	Kway nax? [Why not?]
MUG	Porska. [Because.]
MENCH	Kway nax, Mog? [Why not, Mug?]
NICK	Kway nax, Mog? [Why not, Mug?]
MUG	Porska sue es Sgak. [Because you're a Sgak.]
MENCH	Mog!
NICK	Because I'm a Sgak. What does that mean? Kwel do Sgak mos? [What does Sgak mean?]
MUG	*(poking NICK with his bat)* Sgak mos ee kat vos grute. [Sgak means I hate your guts.]

MUG sniffs and coughs.

	Poo! Kway dis Homelanders fumato see fay? [Why do these Homelanders stink so much?]
MENCH	Sue nax comica, Mog. [You're not funny, Mug.]
MUG	*(trying to lighten things up)* Vancha planch, Mencha? [Want to play, Mench?]
MENCH	Nax. [No.]
MUG	Ay? [What?]
MENCH	Nax! Nax mik sue. [No! Not with you.]

MUG still tries to make MENCH respond, but she pulls away and stands beside NICK.

MUG	Mencha… Mencha. *(then to NICK)* Sgak!

MUG exits.

MENCH	*(to NICK)* Tosta! [Throw the ball!]

NICK   Mench, what does Sgak mean?

MENCH   Kwit? [What?]

NICK   Sorry. Kwel doe Sgak mos? [What does Sgak mean?]

MENCH   Sgak?

NICK   Yo! [Yes!]

            MENCH is very uncomfortable. Silence.

            Well, tell me. Deetmo. [Tell me.]

MENCH   Nax. [No.]

NICK   Kwel doe Sgak mos? [What does Sgak mean?]

MENCH   Ee besta zet nama. [I'd better go now.]

NICK   Look, it's important. Kwel doe Sgak mos? [What does Sgak mean?]

            Pause.

MENCH   Homelander.

NICK   Homelander? Why do they call us that? Kway? [Why?]

MENCH   Porskay chay kat Homelanders. [Because they hate Homelanders.] Ee besta zet nama. [I'd better go now.]

NICK   They hate Homelanders? Kway? [Why?]

            MENCH picks up her sports bag.

MENCH   Tra la. [Bye.]

            She exits.

NICK   It's not fair.

            NICK goes home.

            Dad! Dad!

            MOTHER enters.

	Where's Dad, Mom?
MOTHER	He's at work.
NICK	He's always at work, he's never at home anymore.
MOTHER	You should be happy he has work at all.
NICK	Yeah, but he's not working as a teacher.
MOTHER	No.
NICK	Why not? He is a teacher.
MOTHER	Not in Canada.
NICK	I never get to see him.
MOTHER	I know, neither do I.
NICK	Mom, what's the matter?
MOTHER	I just came back from the store and I'm not going back there. You'll have to do the shopping from now on.
NICK	Why? What happened?
MOTHER	I was leaving the store with my groceries when this man came up and started yelling at me.
NICK	Yelling at you? Why?
MOTHER	I didn't know why and then other people started yelling and pointing.
NICK	What were they saying?
MOTHER	I didn't understand. I got so nervous I dropped the grocery bags, everything spilled on the floor—the eggs, the flour, the milk. They thought I was a fool.
NICK	You're not a fool, Mom.
MOTHER	Maybe they thought I was stupid. I don't know. I didn't understand. I just left all the food there. Oh, I miss Homeland so much, I wish I was there.

NICK   Mom, we haven't been here long. If someone's
            bothering you, just ignore them. Remember, you're
            as strange to them as they are to you, right?

            Pause.

MOTHER   You're right, Nick. I'd better go.

            She starts to go.

NICK   Where?

MOTHER   Back to get my groceries.

NICK   But you don't even know what to say.

MOTHER   You're right. You teach me.

NICK   Okay... Ee gobba may grokos, ee gibba may grund.

MOTHER   What does that mean?

NICK   I'm the idiot who spilled the groceries.

MOTHER   Nick!

NICK   Just kidding, Mom. It really means: "I've come for
            my groceries, give them to me please." Repeat after
            me: Ee gobba may grokos.

MOTHER   *(botching it)* Eee gobble my gekos.

NICK   Grokos.

MOTHER   Grokos.

NICK   Good. Now: Ee gibba may grund.

MOTHER   Giggle my ground.

NICK   No, gibba may grund. Ee gobba may grokos, ee
            gibba may grund.

MOTHER   Ee gobble my grekos, ee giggle my grunt.

NICK   Uh, Mom...

MOTHER   Give me my groceries, I've got a gun.

NICK   Mom!

MOTHER   Just kidding, Nick. Ee gobba may grokos, ee gibba
            may grund.

NICK   Good.

MOTHER   Thanks, Nick.

            MOTHER exits.

NICK   Good luck, Mom.

            *MENCH looks in the window. She has the hockey
            mask on and plays monster, scratching on the glass.
            NICK hears her and goes to the window, calmly
            watches her. Realizing that she has not scared him,
            MENCH takes off the mask. Seeing her face, NICK
            screams and holds his heart. They laugh.*

MENCH   *(holding a basketball)* Sue vancha droob da bolo mik
            mo? [Do you want to dribble the ball with me?]

NICK   Yo, ver shure. [Yes, for sure.]

MENCH   Kitz! [Catch!]

NICK   Gander dis, Mencha. [Look at this, Mench.]

            NICK shows off with the ball.

MENCH   *(taking her turn with the ball)* Gander dis. [Look at
            this.]

            NICK takes the ball, positions to shoot.

NICK   Shotta tobasco? [Should I take a shot?]

MENCH   Yoyo! [Yes!]

NICK   Mo einst. [Me first.]

MENCH   Me doost. [Me second.]

            NICK gets set to shoot. MUG enters.

MUG   Ay, Homer, tosca da glob ta may. [Hey, Homey, toss
            the ball to me.]

MUG grabs the ball away from NICK.

MENCH   Lear corpso. [Drop dead.]

MUG   Nax, ee vancha planch. [No, I want to play.]

> *MUG goes to shoot at the basket, holding the ball over his head. NICK quickly snatches the ball away, holds it behind him so MENCH can take it. She hides it behind her back. MUG whirls around, looking for the ball. He looks at NICK.*

Tosca da glob. [Toss me the ball.]

> *NICK shrugs and shows his empty hands. MUG shoves NICK aside and looks at MENCH, who smiles, revealing the ball and offering it to him. MUG smiles back, figuring he is in control again and that MENCH is back on his side. MUG goes to take the ball from MENCH.*

Gibba may. [Give it to me.]

MENCH   Nax, cue sue tornst. [No, wait your turn.]

> *She tosses the ball over MUG's head to NICK.*

MUG   *(to MENCH)* Chay sue valentino, Mencha? [Is he your boyfriend, Mench?]

> *MUG makes a smooching sound. Then he sniffs:*

Sue fumato como Homelander. [You smell like a Homelander.]

MENCH   Clampit! [Shut up!]

MUG   *(to NICK)* Gibba may da glob. [Give me the ball.]

NICK   Nax, Mog. [No, Mug.]

> *NICK throws the ball through MUG's legs to MENCH.*

MUG   *(to MENCH)* Gibba may. [Give it to me.]

MENCH   Nax vay, row-zhay. [No way, Jose.]

She fakes MUG out a few times with the ball,
making him jump around and then fall to the
ground, then effortlessly tosses it to NICK.

MUG   *(to NICK)* Gibba may! [Give it to me!]

MUG charges at NICK, NICK tries to get the
ball away but MUG has his arm around his
neck, choking him. MENCH runs over and
drags MUG by the hair away from NICK. MUG
grabs MENCH's arm and pulls it around into a
half-nelson. MENCH squirms in pain.

(to NICK) Gibba may. [Give it to me.]

Slight pause. MUG twists harder.

Gibba may. [Give it to me.]

NICK gives MUG the ball. He lets MENCH go.

Taka. [Thank you.]

MUG starts to dribble the ball. Then he stops, turns
to NICK:

Sue vancha planch? [You want to play?]

MUG winds up as if to throw the ball at NICK full
force, then stops, faking him out. Pause. MUG looks
at MENCH. She turns away. MUG hands the ball
to NICK. NICK goes to take it and MUG drops it
on the ground and runs off. Slight pause.

NICK   Es sue bay sue-she? [Are you okay?]

MENCH   Yo. [Yes.]

NICK   Maybe you shouldn't hang around me anymore.

MENCH   Kwit? [What?]

NICK   Me bay shnyden seesaw mik mo nama. [Maybe you
              shouldn't hang around me anymore.]

MENCH   Kway nax? [Why not?]

NICK	Homelanders are dangerous to your health... ee bee Sgak!
MENCH	Gros bos. [Big deal.]
NICK	*(to audience)* I liked her. She was a real friend. *(to MENCH)* Sue vanchen gander me hasa? [You want to see my house?]
MENCH	Nax jesto? [For sure?]
NICK	Kway nax? [Why not?]
MENCH	Kway nax? [Why not?]

They go to NICK's house and enter.

NICK	Mom!

MOTHER enters.

MOTHER	Who's this?
MENCH	Lo, ee be meegro Nick. [Hi, I'm Nick's friend.]
NICK	This is my best friend, Mom.
MOTHER	You didn't tell me you were bringing somebody home.
NICK	She's just my friend. Her name is Mench.
MOTHER	She's Canadian, isn't she?
NICK	Uh huh.
MENCH	Ee noma Mencha. Ee bee ha-ha doe matchay sue. [My name is Mench. I am pleased to meet you.]
MOTHER	Pardon me?
NICK	Chay noma Mencha. Chay bee ha-ha-doe matchay sue. [Her name is Mench. She's pleased to meet you.]
MENCH	Ver shure. [For sure.]
MOTHER	I don't understand.

NICK   Chay noma Mencha, chay bee ha-ha doe matchay
                sue. [Her name is Mench, she's pleased to meet you.]

MOTHER   I don't understand, speak in Homelander to me.

NICK   But I can't with her here. She only speaks English.

MOTHER   Speak Homelander.

NICK   English.

MOTHER   Homelander!

NICK   English!

MENCH   Ee besta zet nama. [I'd better go now.]

                MENCH runs out.

NICK   Nax, Mencha! [No, Mench!] *(to MOTHER)* Good
                work, Mom. Thanks a lot.

MOTHER   I'm sorry, Nick. But I didn't say you could bring a
                Canadian into my house.

NICK   But we live in Canada. My friends are Canadian,
                yours are all Homelanders. Why are you so afraid of
                Mencha? Why wouldn't you speak English with her?

MOTHER   I'll speak English when I want to speak English but
                I don't have to in my own home. Outside we can be
                like them but in here we keep our traditions.

NICK   Does that mean I can't bring my friends home?

MOTHER   You can have Homelander friends here.

NICK   Well, she isn't Homelander and she is my friend. She
                almost got her arm broken standing up for me.

MOTHER   What?

NICK   This bully started picking on me again and she stood
                up to him.

MOTHER   You mean that girl who was just here?

NICK   Yeah.

MOTHER	The Canadian girl stood up for you?
NICK	Yeah, and then he started twisting her arm.
MOTHER	Is she alright?
NICK	Yeah, she is now. Can't you see why I brought her home?
MOTHER	Yes. Of course... I'm sorry, Nick. Look—please—go and bring her in.

NICK runs outside. MENCH has been waiting.

NICK	Mencha. Mencha!
MENCH	Ee bee hee bee. [I'm still here.]
NICK	Co mosto! [Come on!]
MENCH	Ver shure? [Are you sure?]
NICK	Yo yo! [Yeah!]

They go into the house.

MOTHER	Nick, please tell her I'm sorry. Thank her and ask if her arm is alright.
NICK	*(to MENCH)* May momay deetchay taka, et comes bilbo. [My mom says thanks, and wonders how your arm is.]
MENCH	Ee bee banzai. [It's fine.]
MOTHER	*(relieved)* Good.
MENCH	...Good.
MOTHER	*(delighted at her attempt to speak Homelander)* Good!
MENCH	*(delighted at her success)* Good!
NICK	Good!... Her name is Mencha, Mom.
MOTHER	Mencha—please sit down... so you go to school with Nick, Mencha?
MENCH	Good!

MOTHER	…Ask Mencha if she likes school.
NICK	Abba sue lak skoss? [Do you like school?]
MENCH	Skoss? Ee kat skoss. Skoss fumato. Skoss abba may puko! [School? I hate school. School stinks. School makes me puke!]
NICK	…She says it's okay.
MOTHER	Ask her if she wants some of my special pudding.
NICK	Sue vancha globbalos Homelander? Ee bee gusto. [You want some Homelander pudding? It's good.]
MENCH	(politely) Nax, taka. [No, thank you.]
NICK	She says she'd love some.
MOTHER	Good. I'll be right back.

> MOTHER goes to get it. MENCH turns on NICK.

| MENCH | Nick! Taka moosaka! [Nick! Thanks a lot!] |
| NICK | Ee bee gusto gusto. [It's delicious.] |

> MOTHER enters with bowl.

| MOTHER | Here you go, Mencha. |
| MENCH | (hesitantly) Taka. [Thank you.] |

> MENCH smiles at MOTHER then turns to NICK and glares.

| MOTHER | Nick, tell her she doesn't have to eat it if she doesn't like it. |
| NICK | Nax gusto, nax muncho. [If you don't like it, don't eat it.] |

> MENCH stares at him, then smiles at MOTHER. Pause. She smiles at MOTHER again. She looks at the bowl. Takes a little on her spoon. Tastes it. Pause. She does not react. She takes another spoonful. Tastes it. Pause. She instantly wolfs the rest of it down, scraping the bowl with her spoon,

> *then lifting it to lick off the remainder. With her face still in the bowl, she looks up at MOTHER. Slight pause. MENCH puts down the bowl and whispers in NICK's ear. NICK whispers back.*

MENCH   *(haltingly)* Kick me, please.

> *NICK kicks her.*

MOTHER   What?

MENCH   *(more forcefully)* Kick me, please.

> *NICK shrugs, kicks her again.*

MOTHER   Nick!

> *NICK whispers in MENCH's ear.*

MENCH   *(handing MOTHER the bowl)* More, please.

MOTHER   *(delighted)* Come with me.

> *MOTHER and MENCH exit together.*

NICK   *(to audience)* I felt great. Mom liked Mencha and Mencha liked Mom. They got along like, like they were from the same country. But not Mog. He still didn't like me. Whenever he had a chance he'd call me names. And now that I spoke a little English, I knew what he meant and I hated it. And then one day:

> *MUG sneaks to the window and begins writing on it with lipstick. MOTHER enters, sees him.*

MOTHER   Nick!

> *NICK enters, sees him.*

NICK   Mog!

> *MUG runs off.*

MOTHER   Do you know that boy?

NICK   Yeah.

MOTHER   Who is he? Why did he write this?

NICK   He's the one I told you about.

MOTHER   Is this the word, Sgak?

NICK   That's what they call us.

MOTHER   Well, you'd better give me his name.

NICK   No.

MOTHER   Why not?

NICK   I want to work this out myself.

MOTHER   But you could get hurt.

NICK   I know, but he's not the first bully I've ever met. They're everywhere, even in Homeland. Picking on people is an international sport.

MOTHER   So what are you going to do?

NICK   Well, if it's an international sport, I guess I'll just have to play it.

MOTHER   Nick, don't get into trouble.

NICK   ...Okay, Mom.

MOTHER exits.

(to audience) I tried all kinds of things to get Mog to leave me alone.

MUG enters.

MUG   Lo, Sgak. [Hello, Sgak.]

NICK   I wouldn't let it bother me. In fact, I just pretended I liked it. *(to MUG)* Taka, taka. [Thank you, thank you.]

MUG turns away, puzzled.

	I just pretended he was calling me handsome and intelligent.
MUG	Sgak. Sgak!
NICK	*(smiling to MUG)* Taka moosaka. Taka scaree moosh. [Thanks very much. Many big thanks.]

MUG is frustrated and tries again.

MUG	Sgaaaaaaaaaaaaak!!

NICK point inside of MUG's mouth.

NICK	Nax brusho da tooto! [You didn't brush your teeth!]

MUG turns away, holding his mouth. MENCH enters.

MENCH	Nick!
NICK	*(to audience)* Mencha helped.
NICK	Lo. [Hi.]
MENCH	Lo. [Hi.]
NICK	*(asking if she wants to help with MUG)* Yo? [Yes?]
MENCH	*(agreeing to help)* Yo. [Yes.]
NICK	*(to audience)* Sometimes we ignored him.
MUG	Sgak sgakky sgakky sgak, Nick scrunt un Sgak spit. [Nick is a sgakky sgak...]

NICK and MENCH ignore MUG. MUG turns away.

NICK	And once...
MUG	Sgaaak!
NICK	...we just stared right through him.

NICK and MENCH both go bug-eyed at MUG, startling him. MUG turns away.

Once he just happened to bump me.

*MUG walks in a small circle whistling, bumps
NICK.*

So I just happened to bump him back.

*NICK also walks in a circle, whistling, then he
bumps MUG. MUG goes flying.*

And another time...

MUG is swinging his baseball bat.

...we just ran.

*MUG chases MENCH and NICK. At the end of the
chase, NICK stops to face MUG.*

And another time, I just stayed there.

*NICK stands his ground. MUG waves the bat,
threatening to smash NICK, but NICK won't
budge, looking MUG in the eye. Finally MUG
backs down. He lowers the bat and casually plays
with it, as if he had other plans for it altogether,
though he knows he has lost.*

At home, my parents are taking English lessons.
They learned it in a week—well, sort of. I still speak
Homelander. I don't want to forget it. So now I have
two languages, English and Homelander. And Mug?
We're even going to play on the same shlamstick
team.

MENCH hands NICK and MUG hockey sticks.

And you know, I think everything's going to be
okay...

*MUG and NICK get ready to face off. MENCH
blows the whistle. MUG raises the stick high, ready
to smash NICK.*

...maybe.

Invisible Kids

Invisible Kids was first produced by Unicorn Theatre for Children in January, 1985, at the Arts Theatre in London, England, with the following company:

Georgie	Tracy Harper
Vince	George Lascelles
Chris	Anthony Renshaw
Samantha	Josephine Welcome
Thiun	David Forman

Directed by Dennis Foon
Designed by Bernard Culshaw
Lighting by Angus Stewart

Staging Notes

The Playground: Based on the many examples seen throughout the city, the set should be a haphazard collection of platforms, ramps, ladders, ropes and swings. The playground should provide the actors with unlimited possibilities for movement—and yet it should be instantly recognizable to the audience as something they themselves play on every day.

The Music

Pop music that currently stands at the tops of the charts is played at the beginning and end of the show and between the scenes. In this text I indicate the choices that were made for the original production. They are only meant to give an insight into the kind of mood and rhythm I hoped to achieve and should therefore be used only as a guideline—although Bob Marley's "One Love" is a classic that many kids seem to know and adore, so it may continue to be relevant to subsequent productions.

Players
Georgie
Vince
Chris
Samantha
Thiun

They are all about eleven or twelve years old.
Chris is the only child who is meant to be visibly "white."

Setting
A playground in Toronto, present time.

Topicality
It is of extreme importance that every aspect of the production
reflect today's reality. Choices of clothing and music should
be made based on current kids' culture—a quickly evolving
phenomenon. Many of the choices of language and references in
this play will also need constant updating by production theatres
to ensure that the production is in step with the local region and
current trends.

PLEASE NOTE: To acquire a copy of the British version of *Invisible
Kids*, please contact Green Thumb Theatre, 1885 Venables St.,
Vancouver, B.C. V5L 2H6.

Scene One

As the lights come up and the music fades out,
we hear a booming Tarzan ape call. Suddenly,
GEORGIE enters, swinging across the stage on a
rope, howling.

GEORGIE   Jane, Jane, don't worry, I'll save you, don't worry,
girl! AHK! Crocodiles! Take that, you ugly lizard,
you! Stab, stab, stab! I know you're dead 'cause
you're floating with your belly up—belly up means
you're dead meat.

She is attacked by another one.

AH! Jane, Jane, Jane and Boy, calling Jane and Boy,
Jane and Boy come in, Jane and Boy I'm dying, the
crocks got me, Tarzan is dying, the great Tarzan of
the jungle is sinking fast, he's ah, ah, ah...

While GEORGIE has been playing Tarzan,
assuming she was unobserved, VINCE has entered
and has been watching her all the while. He now
interrupts her death scene, making the sound of an
ambulance siren.

VINCE   Whee-uh, whee-uh, whee-uh! Get her on the
stretcher, boys, gotta save Tarzan before he bleeds to
death.

GEORGIE   I'm doing just fine, thank you.

VINCE   We saw the accident, sir. Run over by a green
crocodile. Vicious things.

GEORGIE   I'm not dying, alright?

VINCE   He needs a transfusion, prepare the needle. Tarzan,
old pal, would you mind holding still while we give
you a few gallons of blood?

GEORGIE   I don't want any blood.

VINCE   He's delirious. The fever.

GEORGIE   Vince!

VINCE   Give him a large injection to settle him down. How strong, sir? *(posh voice)* Gorilla strength.

> *VINCE holds GEORGIE down, preparing her for the injection.*

GEORGIE   Vince!

VINCE   ...What?

GEORGIE   Chill out. That's enough.

VINCE   Oh. Sorry, Georgie.

GEORGIE   That's alright, Vince.

VINCE   Thank you, Georgie.

GEORGIE   You're welcome, Vince.

VINCE   Thank you for saying "you're welcome," Georgie.

GEORGIE   That's enough, Vince.

VINCE   Alright, Georgie.

GEORGIE   Alright!... Where's everybody?

VINCE   I don't know. But they'll show up.

GEORGIE   Yes, but when?

VINCE   When they're ready.

GEORGIE   But that means we have to wait.

VINCE   Yes.

GEORGIE   I hate waiting. My mother always says, "be patient, be patient." I feel like I have to be patient so much I'm turning into a patient. They might as well put me into the hospital.

VINCE   I just tried to put you into the hospital, you wouldn't go.... We could count while we wait.

GEORGIE   I hate it! I have to wait for everything. Wait for your friends, wait till you grow up, I even have to wait to see my own big sister.

VINCE   Say what?

GEORGIE   She's still in Jamaica. My parents keep saying one day they'll have enough money to bring her here, but for now I have to wait. Wait, wait, wait.

VINCE   What do you want to count to?

GEORGIE   First one to count to 3,000 is the winner.

VINCE   I have to count to 3,000?

GEORGIE   Or more if it takes that long.

VINCE   Really?

GEORGIE   Yes, 3,000. And maybe more.

VINCE   What comes after 999,999?

GEORGIE   You what?

VINCE   I just want to be sure I know what happens if they take a long, long time to show up.

GEORGIE   One million.

VINCE   One million and one, one million and two…

GEORGIE   Wait, you're supposed to start at one…

VINCE   I can't wait that long, I figure that this way I get a head start. Million and three, million and four…

GEORGIE   You're cheating!

VINCE   I know and you know but they won't know.

GEORGIE   But starting at a million won't make them arrive any faster!

VINCE   Maybe, maybe not.

CHRISTOPHER *enters, eating a sweet.*

Hello, Christopher.

CHRIS   Hi, Vince.

VINCE   Want to count to two million?

GEORGIE   Hi, Christopher!

CHRIS   Hi... *(to GEORGIE)* What are you doing on my ladder?

GEORGIE   It's not your ladder.

CHRIS   Yes, it is.

GEORGIE   It's everybody's ladder.

CHRIS   Get off my ladder, you big...

CHRIS whispers something in her ear.

GEORGIE   You what?

CHRIS   It's my ladder...

GEORGIE   What did you say?

CHRIS   ...Nothing

GEORGIE   I heard what you said!

CHRIS tries to get away, but GEORGIE leaps on his back and starts twisting his head.

CHRIS   Ow, ow, let go of me!

GEORGIE   Not after what you said!

CHRIS   It was a joke!

GEORGIE   That word is no joke!

CHRIS   Vince, Vince, save me, Vince. She's killing me!

VINCE   Alright then.

VINCE doesn't move.

Why are you killing him?

GEORGIE   'Cause he hurt me.

CHRIS   I didn't hurt you.

GEORGIE   Yes, you did.

CHRIS   Ow! Now you're hurting me!

VINCE   He hurts you, now you're hurting me. Does it still hurt?

CHRIS   YES!

GEORGIE   Yes, it still hurts.

CHRIS   It does?

GEORGIE   Yes it does.

CHRIS   Oh.

VINCE   What did he do?

GEORGIE   He called me a name.

CHRIS   So? Everybody calls everybody names.

VINCE   That's true.

GEORGIE   But what if you're a certain colour and they call you…

GEORGIE whispers into VINCE's ear.

VINCE   Get him!

CHRIS runs under a platform. VINCE goes in for the kill.

CHRIS   Hey, come on, hey, it wasn't that bad, people say it all the time. You just don't have a sense of humour… ow, ow…

VINCE   I haven't even hit you yet.

CHRIS   I know, I'm preparing myself. OW!

SAMANTHA enters.

SAM	Hey. Leave him alone.
GEORGIE	No way.
SAM	Fighting's not allowed in the playground.
GEORGIE	Yes, but you don't know what he said.
SAM	Doesn't matter. Fighting is against the rules.
VINCE	But he called her a name... he called her...

VINCE whispers it to SAMANTHA.

SAM	...Thank you. I'm going now to tell Mr. Thomas.
CHRIS	Hey, wait, stop. Don't tell, please, don't tell. I was just kidding. I didn't really mean it.
GEORGIE	But you said it.
CHRIS	It sort of slipped out of my mouth, that's all, like if chewing gum fell out.
GEORGIE	Not the same thing.
CHRIS	I know, I know, it was stupid, alright? It was a mistake. I'll never do it again.
VINCE	Really?
CHRIS	Really.
SAM	Really really?
CHRIS	Really really.
GEORGIE	I don't believe you!
CHRIS	I said I was sorry.
VINCE	He did say that.
GEORGIE	...Alright.
SAM	Well, if that's alright with Georgie, it's alright with me... besides—I have some secret information.
GEORGIE	Secret?

CHRIS	What kind of secret?
SAM	I have secret information from Mr. Thomas.
GEORGIE	What?
CHRIS	What?
VINCE	What?
SAM	It's all on this piece of paper.
GEORGIE	Read it!

Just before she can, THIUN enters.

CHRIS	Hey, hold on. A spy.
GEORGIE	Who's he?
VINCE	I've never seen him before.
SAM	He's the new kid from Vietnam.

VINCE and CHRIS go over to THIUN.

CHRIS	What's your name?
THIUN	Thiun.
VINCE	Are you really from Vietnam?
THIUN	Yes. Hanoi.
CHRIS	How long have you been here?
THIUN	Four year.
VINCE	Where's Hanoi?
THIUN	In North Vietnam.
CHRIS	Oh.
VINCE	You speak English pretty well.
CHRIS	Not that well.
VINCE	That's 'cause he speaks Vietnamese too, right?

THIUN	Right. And Cantonese. And little French.
CHRIS	Really?
THIUN	Yes.
CHRIS	You do not.
GEORGIE	Four languages?
CHRIS	Prove it.
THIUN	How?
SAM	Say something in each language.
THIUN	What?
GEORGIE	Say, "Chris is a big fat Zitbag."
CHRIS	What!
GEORGIE	Say, "Chris is a big ugly Zitbag" in Chinese, Vietnamese and French.
CHRIS	No, no. Say, "Chris is a really handsome and smart guy."

> *THIUN now speaks in each language, using the expression "CHRIS is a human being," or "CHRIS is a good boy." The following are very rough renditions.*

THIUN	*Nay hiho yun.*
GEORGIE	That's Chinese, right?
SAM	That's Vietnamese!
THIUN	That was Cantonese Chinese…. *May lah no ee.*
GEORGIE	That's Vietnamese.
THIUN	Right…. *Ha rosh ee my chik.*
CHRIS	And that's French.
GEORGIE	Didn't sound like French.

THIUN   It was Russian. I know little Russian too.... Chris *c'est bon garcon.*

GEORGIE That's French. Ex.

CHRIS   Where did you learn all that?

SAM   In Vietnam, where else, silly?

CHRIS   Well, he doesn't speak English that well.

THIUN   You speak Vietnamese?

CHRIS   No.

GEORGIE Or Chinese or Russian or French?

CHRIS   No.

GEORGIE Well, when you do, let us know and we'll have a party.

VINCE   *(to THIUN)* That was well wicked, man. Wicked.

THIUN   Wicked?

VINCE   Bad.

THIUN   No good?

VINCE   No, wicked's like bad, that was bad, man. Wicked.

THIUN   Sorry.

GEORGIE No, that was great, Thiun. You speak so many languages, it's totally cool. That's what Vincey meant. Bad and wicked don't mean bad and wicked as if they're really bad and really wicked. Bad and wicked mean good. I mean really good, not really bad or really wicked... really.

THIUN   Good?

GEORGIE Right, good.

THIUN   Wicked.

VINCE   Wicked.

THIUN	Wicked. Now I speak five languages.
GEORGIE	So now that we know he's not a spy, tell us the secret, Samantha.
SAM	Are you ready?
ALL	Yes!
SAM	Alright, then: I was helping in the office so Mr. Thomas let me have this early. These notes won't be going home with you until tomorrow.
GEORGIE	Read it!
SAM	*(clearing her throat)* Notice to parents: Our school is planning to take a group of sixth grade students...
CHRIS	Who? Is that us?
GEORGIE	Who else—read it!
SAM	...on a day trip...
VINCE	Where?
SAM	...to Niagara Falls.
ALL	HOORAY!
GEORGIE	Niagara Falls!
VINCE	Allllright!
SAM	The cost of the trip will be nine dollars.
CHRIS	Nine bucks!
SAM	This includes return bus fare and a ride on the Maid of the Mist.
GEORGIE	That's the boat that goes into the Falls!
VINCE	Niagara Falls!
SAM	Your child is to take a bag lunch and sufficient pocket money for admission to Marineland and the Amusement Park rides.

CHRIS   I'm going on Dragon Mountain for five rides!

SAM   I'm going for ten! Dragon Mountain!

THIUN   Dragon Mountain?

CHRIS   It's a rollercoaster—I hear it goes around in so many loops, people get sick on it, they even fall off and crash and get squashed and die on it.

SAM   I can't wait to try it. I'm going to wear all my Glow Clothes when I go so you can see me like a lightbulb when I'm zooming on the mountain. I'm going to wear my glow yellow top, my glow yellow pants, my glow green socks and my glow pink shoes.

CHRIS   Don't forget your glow pink underpants!

SAM   Shut up!

CHRIS   Take your own advice.

GEORGIE   I just want to see Niagara Falls. I hear they're so big and the water just roars and makes this giant mist so you're like in a cloud and then the sun comes through and makes the most beautiful rainbows.

CHRIS   I just hope my mom can spare the nine bucks. That's a lot of moolah.

THIUN   Moolah?

SAM   *(to THIUN)* He means money.

THIUN   Moolah.

GEORGIE   Are you going, Thiun?

THIUN   I think yes.

SAM   I'm going home to ask right now.

CHRIS   Me too!

GEORGIE   Me three!

SAMANTHA, GEORGIE and CHRIS exit, leaving VINCE and THIUN on stage. VINCE hangs upside down.

VINCE	...Hi.
THIUN	Hi.
VINCE	You like it around here?
THIUN	It's okay.
VINCE	I don't. It's boring around here. Nothing to do. That's why I need a bike.
THIUN	A bike?
VINCE	I really have to get one. A BMX.
THIUN	BMX.
VINCE	Not just your regular BMX. This one's a Hutch. It has Alloy Stem and Full Chrome Plate and Cro-Moly frame and forks.
THIUN	Alloy stem... full chro play...
VINCE	...and Cro-Moly frame forks. I really have to get one. I'm lonely without a bike. You have a bike?
THIUN	I had in Vietnam.
VINCE	You had a bike and you left it there?
THIUN	No room on boat. Very crowded. 100 people on boat as big as this.
VINCE	You'd have to sleep standing up!
THIUN	Right. Sometimes.
VINCE	How long were you on that boat?
THIUN	One, maybe two week. Till it sank.
VINCE	It sank?
THIUN	Yes. Ten people drown. And my mother.

VINCE	That's horrible.
THIUN	Not easy. You go on class trip?
VINCE	Yeah. How about you?
THIUN	Yes. I can speak French there.
VINCE	It'll be great, the ferry and all.
THIUN	Yes.
VINCE	See you then.
	VINCE exits.
THIUN	See you.
	THIUN exits. Blackout. Music.

Scene Two

The lights come up into a half-life. As the music plays, we see THIUN, SAMANTHA and CHRIS enter, take out their lunches and start eating. As the lights fade up, the music fades out. SAMANTHA immaculately sets out a napkin like a little tablecloth and precisely sets out her lunch on it, drawing the attention of CHRIS and THIUN.

SAM	What are you looking at?
CHRIS & THIUN	Nothing.
SAM	Just because you two are slobs doesn't mean I have to be one.

At this moment GEORGIE enters, wearing a surprisingly realistic werewolf mask and gloves. She appears behind SAMANTHA and roars. SAMANTHA shrieks and her lunch goes flying. The others escape up the jungle gym. GEORGIE removes the mask.

Georgette! You made me spill my lunch!

CHRIS   *(scrambling down to see the outfit)* Where'd you get that mask? It's amazing!

GEORGIE   From my big sister.

CHRIS   Can I try it on? Please!

> *She gives it to him, he puts it on and ferociously roars at SAMANTHA, who calmly puts her sandwich inside his shirt. CHRIS stops. Takes off the mask. Feels inside his shirt.*

Oh, gross. *(to GEORGIE)* Where'd you get this thing? This is the best mask in the world.

GEORGIE   From my sister. She makes them.

SAM   She made this? Come on.

GEORGIE   For real. She does makeup. For movies and rock videos and everything.

CHRIS   Could she make me a mask like this?

GEORGIE   Sure she could.

SAM   And me?

GEORGIE   Why not?

CHRIS   I want to be a Transformer. I am Ork the Destroyer.

SAM   She'll make me into a Cat Woman! Shaaa!

> *SAMANTHA claws the air.*

GEORGIE   What do you want to be, Thiun?

THIUN   …Frankenstein.

> *THIUN does a Frankenstein walk.*

CHRIS   When can we get them?

GEORGIE   As soon as she comes to Canada. She's never lived here, she had to wait till my parents had the money 'cause she was grown up, could look after herself. But now we're bringing her here so the whole family can be together again. I'm gonna see my sister.

CHRIS   Hey, Thingy, watch this. Bet they don't do this in Vietnam.

> *CHRIS does some kind of gymnastic feat, perhaps some donkey kicks. THIUN watches, and when CHRIS looks to him, THIUN proceeds to top him, perhaps with a perfectly executed back flip.*

Not bad. But can you do this?

> *Again CHRIS performs a gymnastic move and is totally outclassed by THIUN who brilliantly executes a series of flips. (Important note: THIUN is never showing off, CHRIS is. THIUN never smirks at his success or seems proud of this small victory. He doesn't have to, the others do it for him.)*

But can you do this?

> *CHRIS stands on his head. The others groan. THIUN stands on his head. (Note: on a school tour where this play is performed in gymnasiums, this business may be replaced with hanging upside down on the jungle gym. Replacement lines are indicated in brackets.)*

GEORGIE   Oh, come on, Chris, anybody can do that.

> *GEORGIE now stands on her head as well.*

SAM   I can do it. I can do it too.

> *SAMANTHA tries to stand on her head but is having trouble*

GEORGIE   Come on, Samantha, you can do it.

> *SAMANTHA finally does it too. Now all four are standing on their heads or hanging upside down.*

SAM   I did it, I did it!

>   *VINCE enters. Looks at the group of headstanders/*
>   *hangers without reacting. Then he walks away.*

GEORGIE Hi, Vince.

CHRIS Hi, Vince.

THIUN Hi, Vince.

SAM Hello, Vincent.

VINCE ...Hi.

GEORGIE We're all standing on our heads. [...hanging upside down.]

VINCE Oh.

CHRIS You stand on your head too. [You hang upside down too.]

VINCE Not now, thanks.

GEORGIE Oh, c'mon, Vince.

SAM He doesn't know how. Vincent doesn't know how to stand on his head. [...hang upside down.]

CHRIS He knows how to stand on his head. He always stands on his head. [He knows how to hang upside down. He always knows how to stand upside down.]

GEORGIE What's wrong with you, Vincie?

VINCE Nothing.

GEORGIE *(coming down)* Something's wrong.

>   *The rest begin to come down too.*

CHRIS Something wrong, Vince?

SAM Maybe his mom and dad won't let him go on the class trip.

GEORGIE Is that it, Vincie? Can't you go to Niagara Falls?

VINCE   Yeah, I can go.

THIUN   Something is wrong.

> *VINCE nods.*

GEORGIE   Tell us.

VINCE   Yesterday, after school... walking home. There was the man walking his dog. A German shepherd. He called me a name.

CHRIS   What did he call you?

VINCE   The same thing you called her yesterday.

CHRIS   I said I was sorry. I'll never do it again.

VINCE   I know you won't. But he will.

CHRIS   But you're just a kid.

VINCE   He yelled, "go back to your own country."

GEORGIE   He what?

SAM   But this is your country, you were born here.

CHRIS   Did you tell him? Did you tell him you were born in Canada?

VINCE   I wanted to, but I just kept walking. And then he yelled it again, "go back to where you came from!"... But this is where I come from, this is my home, this is where I have always lived!... He knew that, he didn't care, he didn't like who I was.... Then he took the leash off his big German shepherd and sent it after me.

CHRIS   What!

VINCE   It ran straight for me. Snapping, barking, teeth so big, trying to bite me. So I ran. And it was right behind me.... No! I jumped on top of a car. It just waited. Seemed like hours and it was getting late. My parents would wonder where I was... then it looked like it was sleeping. Just lying there. So I started to climb off the car, quietly, quietly. Crossed the street, if I could just turn the corner, my house was just two streets away…

GEORGIE   Then what?

VINCE   When I got home and told my dad he was furious. He ran out looking for that man but he couldn't find him… I was afraid to go outside.

CHRIS   I could find that man. I'd find him and kill his dog.

GEORGIE   It's not the dog's fault.

SAM   It's the man who trained it. It's the man who sent it after Vincent.

VINCE   It's the man.

CHRIS   Then I'll find the man. And I'll kill him.

GEORGIE   Great, how are you going to do that?

CHRIS   Make a trap. I could do it.

GEORGIE   But what about all his friends? They're just like him. And hurting him would just give his friends an excuse to go after the rest of us.

VINCE   If I had a BMX I could have ridden away from that dog.

GEORGIE   Yeah, if you had a BMX.

SAM   But you don't have one.

VINCE   But if I had one I could have got away.

THIUN   No. Dog is faster. If you run, dog will chase you.

CHRIS   What?

THIUN   Never run from dog.

CHRIS   You mean if a gigantic snarling beast is attacking you, you shouldn't try to get away?

THIUN   No. Never run.

SAM   You are cracked. If a monster drooling dog came after me, I'd run so fast you wouldn't see me.

GEORGIE   Me too.

THIUN   Dog would. Dog faster than you. I show you.

VINCE   What are you going to do?

THIUN   You be Vince. I be dog.

VINCE   What?

THIUN   Ready?

VINCE   For what?

> *THIUN pretends to be a vicious dog and goes for VINCE. He is quite scary.*

Hey, come on now.

THIUN   *(breaking out of dog for an instant in order to coach VINCE)* Don't be afraid. Don't move.

VINCE   What are you doing?

> *THIUN becomes the dog again, totally ferocious. VINCE is terrified, tries to run away but THIUN has him cornered.*

THIUN   Alright. Try again. This time, be still.

VINCE   He's completely crazy.

THIUN   Ready?

> *VINCE hesitates.*

GEORGIE   Go on, Vince.

CHRIS   Yeah.

VINCE   ...Alright then...

> *THIUN comes after VINCE again. Barks like crazy but VINCE does not move. The dog starts to calm down.*

THIUN   You see, you give dog nothing, he has nothing to chase, nothing to bark at, nothing to fear.... You can start to move.

VINCE starts to walk away. THIUN barks madly.

Never turn back on dog.

VINCE   Anything you say, boss.

THIUN   Walk backwards. Slowly.

VINCE moves. THIUN snarls.

Too fast.

VINCE   Sorry, sir.

THIUN   Pretty soon dog let you go.

Finally VINCE escapes.

CHRIS   Is that for real?

GEORGIE Would that really work?

THIUN   Most of time. Some dogs, no, but most dogs stop if you stop. Give them something, they get excited. If nothing to chase, nothing to fight, they stop.

GEORGIE It's my turn. I get to do it too.

SAM   I get to do it too.

SAMANTHA starts barking. The others also turn into dogs and all begin howling. Blackout. Music.

Scene Three

From the blackout the lights fade up into a half-light. We see CHRIS enter, who is trying to jump through one leg. SAMANTHA has also entered. She sits and reads a book. GEORGIE enters and sits apart from the others, obviously upset.

> *THIUN enters and watches CHRIS. The lights fade up full and the music fades out.*

CHRIS   I'm trying to hop through my leg. See, you gotta get this leg through here without letting go, like this. It's really difficult.

> *Holding onto his right foot, CHRIS tries to hop over his right leg with his left foot. He is once again unsuccessful. THIUN holds his right foot, imitating CHRIS.*

Yeah, that's right…

> *THIUN effortlessly hops over his leg.*

Yeah… like that. But—but—can you do this…

> *CHRIS does a cartwheel.*

…with no hands.

> *Slight pause. THIUN flips in the air, performing a cartwheel without using his hands.*

Well, yeah, us… pretty good.

> *VINCE enters. He is beaming with a huge grin.*

What are you smiling at? You think this is funny?

THIUN   Why are you smiling?

VINCE   She said "maybe."

CHRIS   Who said "maybe"?

VINCE   My mom. My mom said "maybe"!

SAM   That's very nice, Vincent. I'm very happy for you that your mother said maybe. Maybe what?

VINCE   Maybe she and Dad will get me that BMX.

CHRIS   No way. The one you want costs two hundred bucks.

THIUN   Lots of moolah.

VINCE	I asked them four hundred times. I asked my dad two hundred times and my mom two hundred and one times.
SAM	That makes four hundred and one.
VINCE	One for good luck.
CHRIS	How long have you been asking them?
VINCE	Forever. I've been asking them for a BMX forever.
SAM	And in total you have asked them four hundred and one times.
VINCE	Yesterday.
SAM	What?
VINCE	I asked them four hundred and one times yesterday. And I told them that I am going to ask them four hundred times a day until they get me a BMX. That's when Mom said "Maybe."
SAM	I can see why.
CHRIS	They'll never buy you one.
VINCE	Maybe.
CHRIS	They just said "maybe" to shut you up.
VINCE	Maybe.
CHRIS	They don't have the money. They'll never buy you a BMX in a million years.
VINCE	Maybe.
CHRIS	They won't send you on the class trip and buy you a BMX.
VINCE	Maybe.
CHRIS	Stop saying "maybe"!
VINCE	Maybe.

CHRIS	Aaaargh!
SAM	I'm going on the class trip. I wouldn't miss it for the world. I'm going to ride the roller coaster five times. No, ten times. Did you bring your permission slips? Today is the deadline.
CHRIS	Yeah, I did.
VINCE	Me too.
THIUN	Me three.
SAM	What about you, Georgie?

GEORGIE is silent.

	Wouldn't your parents give you the money?
GEORGIE	Yeah, they would.
SAM	So are you going or not?
GEORGIE	I don't care.
CHRIS	What do you mean you don't care?
GEORGIE	I don't care if I go or not. I don't care about nothing.
SAM	That doesn't make sense. Nothing's nothing, so you can't care about nothing because nothing is nothing.
CHRIS	What are you talking about?
SAM	Nothing.
GEORGIE	Well, it is about something.
SAM	See, I told you!
GEORGIE	My big sister can't come to Canada for two years.
VINCE	I thought she was coming right away.
CHRIS	She's supposed to turn me into a Transformer.
SAM	What happened? Doesn't she want to live here?

GEORGIE   Yeah, but they're making her wait two years for her papers. The ones that say she's allowed to live in Canada.

CHRIS   But you live here, your whole family lives here. Why are they making her wait?

THIUN   Much paperwork. Not easy.

GEORGIE   It's easy if you're from England or France or Switzerland. My dad says people from Europe only have to wait two months.

CHRIS   What?

GEORGIE   But if you're from India or South America or Africa you have to wait a year or a year and a half or two years or even longer.

CHRIS   What?

VINCE   'Cause we're the wrong colour, that's what!

CHRIS   But I want Georgie's sister to come. She's gonna make us masks. She's gonna transform me.

SAM   Well, you have to wait, that's all. They just don't have enough workers in the offices to do the work faster.

VINCE   They do in France.

SAM   Well, that's too bad, isn't it? That's just the way it is.

GEORGIE   It's not fair.

CHRIS   I can't stand this. I want to do something. I'm going to beat somebody up. Tell me who is making this happen, Georgie, I'm going to find that jerk and smash his face in.

SAM   Yeah, you and whose army? It's not just one person, it's the government of Canada.

CHRIS   You mean, like in Ottawa?

    SAMANTHA nods yes.

So what are we going to do?

VINCE   ...Let's make a petition.

THIUN   A petition? For people to sign?

VINCE   Yes.

CHRIS   What'll we say on it?

VINCE   We'll say we do not think it is fair for some people to only wait two months when Georgie's sister has to wait two years.

GEORGIE   Not just my sister, everybody. We should all be treated the same.

VINCE   We should all be treated the same.

CHRIS   Good.

THIUN   Wicked.

CHRIS   Alright, Georgie?

GEORGIE   Alright. Who are you going to send it to?

VINCE   After we get, say, a thousand kids to sign, we'll send it to, to...

CHRIS   Bryan Adams.

SAM   You're really sad, you know that, Christopher? You have to send it to somebody who can do something. You have to send it to the Prime Minister.

GEORGIE   Brian Mulroney?

CHRIS   He'd never listen to us.

VINCE   Maybe.

SAM   He might do something.

GEORGIE   Maybe... something.

> *GEORGIE plays Mr. Mulroney.*

Good morning, Christopher, nice to have you in the beautiful city of Ottawa. Oh, a petition, give it here, I know just what to do with that.

She grabs the imaginary papers from CHRIS and tosses them away.

Oh, what happened here, son? Is that a bit of chocolate smeared around you lip? You know it's not very Canadian to have a dirty face.

CHRIS   The petition, Mr. Mulroney, the petition.

GEORGIE Thank you, Christopher, I have given it to the proper authorities. Now go wash your face.

CHRIS   Aaaaargh!

GEORGIE And don't forget behind the ears.

Mr. Mulroney waves goodbye with a big TV smile.

CHRIS   He won't listen to us, we're just kids.

THIUN   Put on TV.

CHRIS   Right, we'll take it to the CBC, to "The Journal".... Hello, this is Barbara Frum! A special bulletin has just come in:

SAMANTHA makes a bomb sound, dropping the bulletin into his hand.

A large gang of angry schoolkids have been seen protesting. They are considered to be dangerous... and armed.

All wave their arms.

VINCE   And legged! *(He waves his legs.)* ...But we could... we really could.

CHRIS   Well, why not? Why shouldn't we? We don't have to be invisible.

GEORGIE Right.

CHRIS   And we won't go on the trip because we'll be too busy making petitions.

VINCE   Yes!

CHRIS   We can go to Niagara Falls any old time. Georgie's sister has to come to Canada now.

THIUN   Right!

GEORGIE   You sure?

CHRIS   Sure we're sure.

VINCE   Yeah.

THIUN   Yeah.

CHRIS   Yeah.

They all look at SAMANTHA. She looks away. Slight pause. Blackout. Music.

Scene Four

The lights come up to a half-light. GEORGIE and THIUN enter, working on the petitions. The lights fade up to full, the music fades out.

GEORGIE   Oh, no!

THIUN   What is it?

GEORGIE   This is the 25th petition I've prepared to be signed.

THIUN   Good.

GEORGIE   But I think I spelled the Prime Minister's name wrong.

THIUN   Let me see… M-A-L-O-O-N-Y. That spells Maloony. I think you are right. This is wrong.

GEORGIE   Maloony. I knew it.

THIUN   Sorry.

GEORGIE   Now I have to do all of these over again.

THIUN   I'll help you.

GEORGIE   Thanks.

> CHRIS and VINCE enter.

CHRIS   Got any more petitions ready? Look at all the ones
               filled out so far.

VINCE   Two hundred names.

GEORGIE   Any doubles?

CHRIS   Doubles?

GEORGIE   People who have signed twice. Or three times. Or
               four times.

CHRIS   Ah, no. Nobody's signed these four times.

GEORGIE   Let me look... Christohper, this page is all
               your signature. You signed it thirty-five times.
               Christopher Welch, Christopher Welch, Christopher
               Welch.

CHRIS   I was only trying to help.

GEORGIE   Well, you're not.

CHRIS   So I made a mistake.

GEORGIE   A big one.

> GEORGIE tears up the paper.

CHRIS   Wait! Don't!

GEORGIE   It's not good for anything.

CHRIS   I was going to give it to my mom. I've never signed
               my name that many times in a row before. I thought
               she might like to put it on the fridge.

GEORGIE   *(giving him the pieces)* Get some scotch tape and it'll be as good as new… and don't do it again.

CHRIS   Alright.

VINCE   We told Mr. Thomas why we weren't going on the trip.

THIUN   Was he unhappy with us?

VINCE   No, he understood. He said he respected us, said it showed we were serious. And he signed the petition.

SAMANTHA enters.

CHRIS   But he's not postponing the whole trip?

GEORGIE   Why should he?

CHRIS   He'd have to postpone it if nobody would go.

GEORGIE   He'd just send the bus, the bus driver, and Samantha.

SAM   I'm not the only one going. A lot of us are going. Just because you aren't going doesn't mean I shouldn't.

CHRIS   But you should help us. What's happening to Georgie's sister isn't fair.

SAM   I know it's not fair—but why should I suffer too?

VINCE   Because next time it could be youuuu!

SAM   But I want to go to Niagara Falls.

THIUN   Everybody does.

SAM   Well, you can do what you want. I want to go on the Maid of the Mist. I want to go on that Dragon Mountain Rollercoaster. I want to wear my glow shirt and pants and jacket.

CHRIS   It's still not fair.

SAM   I don't care. I won't miss it. I'm going to go. I'm going.

Slight pause. SAMANTHA exits.

CHRIS   The creep.

GEORGIE   I don't blame her.

CHRIS   What? You don't blame her?

GEORGIE   No. If I were in her shoes, I'd probably go too.

VINCE   Really?

GEORGIE   Yeah. I want to go. I'm dying to see the Falls. I want to see how it makes rainbows. I mean, look at you guys. You just want a chance to yell about something. And all Vince cares about is getting a stupid BMX anyway. You don't care about going.

CHRIS   That's not true. I want to go.

GEORGIE   Then go. Don't let me stop you.

CHRIS   But I'm not going.

GEORGIE   Well you should. You should go to Niagara Falls. Go home and tell your moms and dads you've changed your mind. The bus is leaving early so go home and get some sleep. Go on!

CHRIS   What's with her?

THIUN   She is sad. She wants to go on the trip.

GEORGIE   They don't want us in this country. If they did, we wouldn't have to fight for our rights all the time. My sister's waited so long to be with us again and now we finally have the money and they're making her wait longer. They don't care. Neither did that man who put his dog on you, Vince. All they know is that we're a different colour than them and they don't like us.

CHRIS   I'm a different colour than you and I like you.

GEORGIE   Thanks, but what about the rest of them?

CHRIS   We'll keep working like this with the petitions and
          other stuff. Maybe they'll change.

GEORGIE   *(cynically)* Maybe.

VINCE   Maybe.

THIUN   Maybe.

VINCE   If I only had a BMX. I'd take the petitions and
          deliver them on my bike right to the CBC.

GEORGIE   Your dad wouldn't let you ride it there.

VINCE   Of course he would. For something like this.

CHRIS   But you're never gonna get a BMX, so why worry
          about it?

VINCE   I could. I might.

GEORGIE   He's right. Why worry about it. We can't do
          anything. And first thing in the morning, Samantha
          gets to go to Niagara Falls all dressed up in her Glow
          Clothes.

CHRIS   She'll have so much Glow stuff on she'll turn
          radioactive.

VINCE   Let's get some more petitions signed.

THIUN   Good idea.

CHRIS   Come on, Georgie. There's lots to do.

GEORGIE   Okay…. Dear Prime Minister, Dear Prime Minister…

          CHRIS looks at the petitions.

CHRIS   Brian Maloony…. Who's Brian Maloony?

          Blackout. Music.

Scene Five

*Lights fade up to half-light. THIUN, GEORGIE
and CHRIS are counting petitions. Lights come up
full, music fades out.*

THIUN   ...Five hundred seven... five hundred eight...

CHRIS   Five hundred and eight. That's amazing. We got five
hundred and eight people to sign these things. That
is very impressive. I am impressed.

GEORGIE   Yeah, so? Nothing is going to happen. Mulroney
won't do anything and Samantha will be back any
minute all glowing from Niagara Falls and all we
did was waste our time.

CHRIS   We're not wasting our time. Something might
happen.

GEORGIE   What? This stuff won't get past his secretary. It'll
go straight in the rubbish bin and then you'll have
nothing.

THIUN   Not so. I have these to Mr. Thomas. He made copy
of all petitions. Now we have two copies, see? Both
in envelopes. Look at address.

GEORGIE   *(reading)* The Prime Minister, House of Commons,
Ottawa... What's the other one say? To CBC TV, 250
Front St. East, Toronto, Ontario.... Maybe they will
do something.

CHRIS   Where's Vince? I thought he wanted to deliver this
stuff.

GEORGIE   Waiting for his BMX, I guess.

CHRIS   Poor sucker. He'll never get one. Let's chip in for his
bus fare.... Here's a dime.

THIUN   Here's some...

*SAMANTHA enters. She is wearing her Glow
Clothes.*

GEORGIE   Well, look who's back—the world traveller.

CHRIS   My sunglasses, my sunglasses, you're blinding me!

THIUN   Hi.

GEORGIE   How was the trip?

SAM   Do you really want to know?

CHRIS   Did you go on Dragon Mountain?

SAM   'Course.

GEORGIE   Well, tell us what happened, it's the least you can do.

SAM   We took the bus to Niagara Falls. And then we came back. That's all. We went to some shops. Ate candy and chocolate and drank Coke.

CHRIS   Chocolate?

SAM   Yeah. Here, I brought you some back.

CHRIS   Thanks!

>   *CHRIS grabs the candy and starts to eat, then notices the others eyeing him. He sheepishly passes the bag around.*

GEORGIE   *(to SAM)* Well, go on.

SAM   Then we went to a souvenir shop. The other kids bought little key rings with waterfalls on them but I wouldn't waste my money. I was saving it for Dragon Mountain.

GEORGIE   Did you go?

SAM   Then we saw the Falls.

GEORGIE   What're they like?

SAM   Huge. Gigantic. You stand on top and look down at them and the mist is everywhere.

GEORGIE   Did you see the rainbow?

SAM   No, it was cloudy. You only get the rainbow if the
           sun shines on the mist. It was just very damp.

GEORGIE   Too bad.

SAM   Then we went on the *Maid of the Mist*. That's the boat
           that takes you underneath the Falls.

GEORGIE   I know.

SAM   I got soaking wet, I was freezing. So I ate more
           chocolates to warm myself up.

CHRIS   You have any more of those?

SAM   Here. Take it all.

CHRIS   Thanks!

           CHRIS gorges on the chocolates.

GEORGIE   And then what happened?

SAM   Nothing.

CHRIS   Didn't you go on Dragon Mountain? On the roller-
           coaster.

SAM   Uh-huh.

CHRIS   How many times did you go? Six? Seven?

SAM   ...Once.

CHRIS   Just once?

GEORGIE   Once?

THIUN   Once?

SAM   I got on it and was so excited, I couldn't wait to get
           on top and glow. There were three loops, four loops,
           I couldn't wait. Some kids were afraid to go but I
           wasn't. I had enough money to go ten times. Finally
           it started, kind of slow at first as it goes up the
           mountain and up to the top of the first loop and then
           it goes screaming down.

CHRIS   Was it great?

SAM   I don't know. I felt sort of funny.

CHRIS   *(as he eats a chocolate)* Why?

SAM   I was too excited to eat all day except for those
             chocolates. I could really feel them in my stomach.

CHRIS   The chocolate?

SAM   Yeah, the chocolate.

CHRIS   Oh.

SAM   Then we started going up the second loop. I could
             see everybody way down below and the seagulls
             were flying around my head...

THIUN   Nice.

SAM   I started feeling dizzy. I started turning green. And
             then at the top of the loop...

CHRIS   What?

SAM   *(whispering)* ...I threw up.

CHRIS   Ohhhhh...

SAM   I don't know how I finished the ride. I thought I was
             going to die. I thought I was dead. I've never been so
             sick in my whole life.

GEORGIE   Still, it was fun to see Marineland and the Falls and
             everything.

SAM   I don't remember. I was too sick.

THIUN   Welcome home.

SAM   Thanks.... I should have stayed home. Stayed with
             you guys.... Sorry.

GEORGIE   That's alright. Somebody had to go. At least we
             know what we missed.

CHRIS   Oh, gag. I never want to eat chocolate again.

        VINCE enters. He is wearing a BMX jacket.

VINCE   Hi.

ALL   Hi, Vince.

VINCE   I'm ready to take the petitions to the post office and the CBC.

CHRIS   Good. We've put together the bus fare for you.

VINCE   I don't need it.

CHRIS   What, planning to walk?

VINCE   No. I went home last night and my mom and dad were standing there and they had this funny look on their faces. I didn't know what was up. Then my dad says to me, "I got a riddle for you: what's got an alloy stem, fully chrome plate and cro-moly frame and forks?" I said, "only one thing's got alloy stem, full chrome plate and cro-moly frame and forks." So he said, "Next Christmas, all you get is a stocking and on your birthday all you get is a cake." And I said, "Why?" And he said, "Because all your presents are right here now." And there it was.

        The lights change into magical colours. The "Star Wars" theme plays. Slowly, incredibly, a glowing BMX appears, perhaps from the sky.

VINCE   My own bike. My own BMX.

        It touches the ground. He sits on it.

It's beautiful. It's mine.

        He drives it, performs a few stunts.

I can do wheelies and bronkies and table tops. My bike! My BMX!

        The lights return to normal. The kids are in awe.

CHRIS   Can I ride it? Can I ride it!

VINCE   First ride is for the person who is delivering the petitions.

SAM   Who?

> *VINCE goes to GEORGIE and puts a helmet on her. She shakes hands all around.*

CHRIS   Here are the petitions. This one is for the post office, special delivery to Ottawa, and this one goes straight to the CBC. Good luck.

> *GEORGIE joins VINCE on the bike. He adjusts his visor. She taps him on the helmet. The others cheer and wave goodbye as they exit.*

THIUN   He got his BMX.

CHRIS   I don't believe it.

SAM   Do you think it'll work?

CHRIS   You mean, Mr. Mulroney, will he do anything?

THIUN   Maybe. Maybe not.

CHRIS   At least we're doing something.

SAM   Right. *(reaching into her pocket)* Oh, Christopher, do have some more chocolate.

CHRIS   Aaaaaaaaaaaargh.

> *Blackout. Music: Bob Marley's "One Love."*

photo by Elizabeth Dancoes

Dennis is the co-founder of Vancouver's acclaimed Green Thumb Theatre and served as artistic director for twelve years. As a playwright, his body of plays continues to be produced internationally in numerous languages. Dennis has received the British Theatre Award, two Chalmers Canadian Play Awards, the Jesse Richardson Career Achievement Award, and the International Arts for Young Audiences Award. He's won a Gemini, two WGC Awards, three Leos, and a Robert W. Wagner Award for his screenplays. Dennis wrote the screenplay for the feature film *Life Above All*, Prix François Chalais winner at the 2010 Cannes Film Festival, 2011 Academy Award Shortlist for Best Foreign Language Film, and a Leo winner for Best Screenplay.

Originally published by Pulp Press, 1989.
First Playwrights Canada Press edition: September 2006.
Third printing: March 2014.
Printed and bound in Canada by Imprimerie Gauvin, Gatineau

Front Cover painting, *Be Left Alone* and design by Derek von
Essen.
Production Editor: MZK

PLAYWRIGHTS CANADA PRESS
202-269 Richmond St. W.
Toronto, ON
M5V 1X1

416.703.0013
info@playwrightscanada.com
www.playwrightscanada.com